Food Chains and Webs

Grassland
Food Chains

Angela Royston

Heinemann
LIBRARY

Chicago, Illinois

Edited by Claire Throp, Diyan Leake, and
Helen Cox Cannons
Designed by Joanna Malivoire and
Philippa Jenkins
Original illustrations © Capstone Global
Library Ltd 2014
Picture research by Elizabeth Alexander and
Tracy Cummins
Production by Victoria Fitzgerald
Originated by Capstone Global Library Ltd
Printed in the United States of America in
North Mankato, MN. 112014 008649RP

**Library of Congress Cataloging-in-
Publication Data**
Royston, Angela, 1945- author.
  Grassland food chains / Angela Royston.
    pages cm.—(Food chains and webs)
  Includes bibliographical references and index.
  ISBN 978-1-4846-0522-6 (hb)—ISBN
978-1-4846-0529-5 (pb) 1. Grassland
ecology—Juvenile literature. 2. Food chains
(Ecology)—Juvenile literature. 3. Grassland
animals—Juvenile literature. 4. Wildlife
conservation—Juvenile literature. I. Title.
  QH541.5.P7
  577.4—dc23   2013040546

Acknowledgments
We would like to thank the following for
permission to reproduce photographs: Alamy
pp. 11c, 25 grass (© Danita Delimont), 13 (©
Patrycja Loeppky), 14 (© Thomas Kitchin &
Victoria Hurst), 16, 23b (© blickwinkel), 17c (©
imagebroker), 19 (© Arco Images GmbH), 20 (©
sam oakes), 21 (© fStop), 22 (© Dave Zubraski),
23a (© FLPA), 23c (© Naturfoto-Online), 24,
25 bison (© Cultura RM), 25 chicken (© Scott
Camazine), 25 ferret (© All Canada Photos), 26
(© James Prout), 27 (© Ron Niebrugge), 28 (©
AgStock Images, Inc.), 29 (© Dennis Frates);
Getty Images pp. 8 (Magdalena Biskup Travel
Photography), 9 (Tier Und Naturfotografie J und
C Sohns), 25 cricket (National Geographic);
Shutterstock pp. 1 (© Sam Dcruz), 4 (© summer.
wu), 5 (© Andrzej Kubik), 7 (© tandemich), 10
(© John Wollwerth), 11a, 25 hawk (© Stephen
Mcsweeny), 11b, 25 prairie dog (© l i g h t p o e
t), 12 (© Mazzzur), 15, 25 coyote (© creative), 17a
(© Peter Betts), 17b (© erichon), 18 (© Francois
Loubser), 23d (© Johan van Beilen), 23e (© Smit).

Cover photograph of zebras in Tanzania
reproduced with permission of Shutterstock
(© Jeeri).

We would like to thank Michael Bright for his
invaluable help in the preparation of this book.

Every effort has been made to contact copyright
holders of material reproduced in this book.
Any omissions will be rectified in subsequent
printings if notice is given to the publisher.

All the Internet addresses (URLs) given in this
book were valid at the time of going to press.
However, due to the dynamic nature of the
Internet, some addresses may have changed,
or sites may have changed or ceased to
exist since publication. While the author and
publisher regret any inconvenience this may
cause readers, no responsibility for any such
changes can be accepted by either the author
or the publisher.

Contents

Some words are shown in bold, **like this.**
You can find out what they mean by
looking in the glossary.

What Is a Grassland?

A grassland is a huge area of land that is mostly covered by grass. Flowers grow there, too, but with only a few shrubs and trees.

Flowers grow on grasslands in Asia.

Elephants and zebras graze on grasslands in Africa.

Many kinds of animals live on grasslands, from huge elephants and bison to insects such as butterflies. This books looks at how grassland animals find food and survive.

Where Are the Grasslands?

This map shows the biggest areas of grassland in the world. Many grasslands have been taken over by farmers to grow wheat, corn, and other crops.

Grasslands are marked on the map in dark green.

North American prairies

Asian steppes

The Equator

African savanna

Australian bush

South American pampas

Wild horses roam freely on the steppes in Mongolia.

Grasslands have different names in different parts of the world. These include prairies, pampas, steppes, savannah, and bush. The coldest grasslands are the Asian steppes.

What Is a Food Chain?

Living things need **energy** to move and to survive. Their energy comes from food.

Kangaroos need lots of energy to bound across the land.

A cheetah is the fastest runner in the world.

A **food chain** shows how plants and animals are linked by food. It also shows how energy passes from one living thing to another.

A Prairie Food Chain

This **food chain** comes from the prairies of North America. It shows how a prairie dog is linked to the grass and to a hawk. The prairie dog eats grass to get **energy**. The hawk gets energy by eating the prairie dog. Without the grass, both animals would starve.

The prairies in South Dakota

Food chain

A hawk swoops down and grabs a prairie dog

Prairie dogs feed on grass

Grass grows on a North American prairie

Plants and the Sun

Food chains begin with plants, because all green plants make their own sugary food. Plants are called **producers**.

Some wheat grows wild on the prairies.

Sugar made in the leaves feeds the flowers.

Plants make sugar in their green leaves. Sugary liquid is taken to every part of the plant. It also feeds any animal that eats the plant.

Animal Consumers

Animals are called **consumers** because they consume plants or other animals. Some animals, such as prairie dogs and many caterpillars, eat only plants. They are called **herbivores**.

A caterpillar eats leaves and grows bigger and bigger.

A coyote eats almost everything, from plants to insects and deer.

Hawks are **carnivores**, because they eat only meat from other animals. Some animals, such as coyotes, eat plants and meat. They are called **omnivores**.

A Savannah Food Chain

Many large animals live on the African savannahs. In this **food chain**, the zebras are **herbivores** and the lions are **carnivores. Energy** passes from the grass through the zebras to the lions.

African grasslands are called savannah.

Food chain

Lions watch the zebras, waiting for a chance to attack one

Zebras graze on the grass

Grass grows on an African savannah

Top Predators

Lions and hyenas are at the top of their **food chains**, because no animal hunts them. **Carnivores** often prey on old, sick, or young animals. They pick off the weakest animals, because they are the easiest to catch.

Hyenas usually hunt together in clans.

A golden eagle is a top predator and a scavenger in many grasslands.

Hyenas and many other **predators** are also **scavengers**. Scavengers feed on dead animals.

Feeding on Waste

Scavengers, such as vultures, pick the rotting flesh off dead animals, leaving only clean bones. Decomposers go even further.

Vultures wait for the lion to finish her meal before they feed on the leftovers.

A mushroom has no leaves. It grows from tiny root-like strands in the soil.

Decomposers include mushrooms, worms, and many insects. They feed on waste in droppings and the remains of dead plants and animals. As they feed, they break up the waste into tiny pieces, which become part of the soil.

A Meadow Food Chain

Grasslands do not have to be really large. A meadow is a large, grassy field. In this **food chain**, **energy** passes from the flowers through the hoverfly to the spider, the lizard, and the fox. The fox is an **omnivore** that snatches up the lizard, but also feeds on plants.

This meadow is in Great Britain.

Food chain

The fox pounces on the lizard

The lizard snaps up the spider

The spider catches the hoverfly

The hoverfly finds food in the flower

The flower grows in the meadow

Food Webs

The diagram on page 25 shows how different **food chains** link together to form a **food web.** If all the possibilities were included here, it would include most of the plants and animals in a **habitat!**

Bison feed on shrubs as well as on grass.

Food web

hawk

coyote

black-footed ferret

prairie dog

prairie chicken

bison

cricket

grass and plants

Key Links

Some animals or plants are particularly important to a **habitat**. Many animals rely on them, and they are key links in **food chains**.

A pronghorn likes living close to prairie dogs.

Burrowing owls nest in the prairie dogs' tunnels.

A prairie dog is a key link. Ferrets, golden eagles, and hawks hunt prairie dogs. Bison and pronghorn like to graze on grass that has been clipped by prairie dogs.

Protecting Food Chains

People cause the greatest harm to **food chains.** Huge areas of grasslands are used to grow crops, such as wheat and corn.

Much of the prairie land in North America is used to grow wheat.

Prairie animals are protected in Badlands National Park.

Farmers have killed so many prairie dogs that black-footed ferrets have almost died out. They now survive in national parks, where prairie plants and animals are safe from people.

Glossary

carnivore animal that eats only the meat of other animals

consumer living thing, particularly an animal, that feeds on other living things, such as plants and other animals

decomposer living thing, such as an earthworm, fungus, or bacterium, that breaks up the remains of plants and animals and turns them into soil

energy power needed to do something, such as move, breathe, or swallow

food chain diagram that shows how energy passes from plants to different animals

food web diagram that shows how different plants and animals in a habitat are linked by what they eat

habitat place where something lives

herbivore animal that eats only plants

omnivore animal that eats plants and animals

predator animal that hunts other animals for food

producer living thing, such as a plant, that makes its own food

scavenger animal that feeds off the flesh and remains of dead animals

Find Out More

Books

Facthound offers a safe, fun way to find web sites related to this book. All the sites on Facthound have been researched by our staff.

Here's all you do:

Visit www.facthound.com

Type in this code: 9781484605226

Web sites

www.blueplanetbiomes.org/prairie.htm
This web site has information about different habitats, or biomes, including the North American prairies.

environment.nationalgeographic.com/environment/ habitats/grassland-profile/
This National Geographic web site includes facts about grasslands as well as links to related topics such as threats to grasslands.

worldwildlife.org/habitats/grasslands
The World Wildlife Fund web site has a section on grasslands and the animals that live there.

Index